I0597364

Tilde

A LITERARY JOURNAL

~

Vol. 3 Issue 2 ~ Winter 2021
An Imprint of Thirty West Publishing House

EDITOR-IN-CHIEF

Josh Dale

MANAGING EDITOR	TE Tomaino
POETRY EDITOR	Carrie Soltner
FICTION EDITOR	Nick McMenamin
NON-FICTION EDITORS	Bob Kaplan
	Melissa DiGiovannantonio
COVER PHOTOGRAPHY	Connor Doyle

Tilde: A Literary Journal
Vol. 3 Issue 2~ Winter 2021

www.thirtywestph.com

ISBN-13:	978-1-7345158-6-2
ISSN (Print):	2576-960x
ISSN: (Online):	2576-9618

CONTENTS

EDITOR'S NOTE

Well…well…well…It's about time they let the Nonfiction Editor speak. Usually, they keep me under the stairs like Harry Potter. No, that's not true—at least Harry Potter had clothes. But as fate would have it, this particular issue of *Tilde* features Nonfiction. Honestly, I couldn't be happier. Sure, I used to love poetry and fiction, just like everyone else. Then it all changed for me during my last year at college, when a professor made me fall in love with Creative Nonfiction through the pieces we studied. Now I can now go on and on about Kristine Ervin, but this *is* the Editor's Note, isn't it? I've been editing for so long that I can't remember the last time I published something of my own—I better not blow this…Where was I? Ah, yes, I could discuss that final year of college. That discovery and exploration of Creative Nonfiction, which, years later, I would devote a portion of my life to. However, I would rather gush over the pieces in the very issue that you are reading right now.

As *Tilde* pushes on, the assortment of submissions received have become more and more diverse. At first, I would find myself reviewing tons of recycled college essays—Word from the wise, just because you got a "B" in your English 101 course, doesn't mean your final term paper is Creative Nonfiction. But as you can see by this issue, that has changed. CNF has grown over the years. Not to mention it used to have one editor, but now has two. For Winter 2021, the general theme throughout *Tilde* deals with the past and the different origins people have. In "Imposter" Michelle Spences-Lee asks and answers the question: *"Where am I from?"* as Capella Parrish does in "Still Standing" while telling stories about her difficult relationship with her father. In "85 Minutes" David Oliver gives us a creative yet awkward narrative through a series of text messages—leading to a monumental sexual escapade. Daniel Brawand provides an eye-opening glimpse into what it's like being a newly transitioned trans man in "Masks We Can't Remove" while Victoria England's "What I said Hiking a Slot Canyon in Big Bend Ranch State Park" is a very humorous and crude memory written as a list. "Heart" by Mara Adamitz Scrupe contributes to a *Tilde* "first" by bringing a personal album to a larger audience with photos and text. And, finally, in "Bless the Rain" Renee Nicholson discusses her long history with the band Weezer in reflections of former and present life. All these pieces discuss and question the past. They address both origin and identity. In my opinion, this is the perfect theme for a Creative Nonfiction-focused issue of *Tilde*.

We all come from somewhere. We may not know where we're going, but we know where we've been. Yet somehow the past is still shaded with mystery.

Now, as much as I am grateful and proud of the team we have here at *Tilde*, I would love to mention everyone and thank them in great detail for their work and support over the years, but there just isn't time or space. But I cannot wrap this Editor's Note up without thanking one person—as the CNF selection in this journal would not exist without her. That person is Melissa DiGiovannantonio. Not only does she have the longest last name, but also the biggest heart. I have known Melissa for many years, and we have even travelled around the country together—Well... it was just Texas, but we still bonded. Melissa is not only the most qualified person to help me comb through submissions and edit selections in Creative Nonfiction, but she's also the only person who can keep me in line. This is mainly because of how much I respect her, and partly because she scares me a little bit...

I change my mind. We have a great team, and I'm going to thank them all. If you have a problem with it, then just skip ahead to the good part of the magazine. But, thank you: TE Tomaino, Nick McMenamin, Carrie Soltner, and, most of all, Josh Dale. Thank you all for putting up with my crap for all these years.

The last thing I would like to mention is that I have never read a single Harry Potter book, nor have I seen any of the movies. The fact that he lives under the stairs is all I know. But how much different is it from running the CNF genre of a printed literary journal? *Abra kadabra!* He says that…right?

—BK

BENJAMIN BARTU

KRUBERA

so pale,

      this descendant light—

the creatures beady-blind

and shrivelsome. the sediment

lining the caves

    older than we'd ever be—

the spiders of children.

I didn't know time could stretch a thing

so colorless

and thin. they say everything went pear-shaped

i guess. slipped under the starry

sinkwater.

    put back

in the refrigerator.

the kind that for all you know stays lit

long after you close the door.

It's the mid-1990s, and after college I take marketing jobs I don't like for disappointing pay, working for white, former frat boys who weren't as smart, witty, or good-looking as they imagined themselves to be. I try to ooze cool, with my long hair cut into a sleek, short bob stacked in the back and wear cat-eye sunnies that match with cat-eyeliner, plaid skirts, GAP tees, and cardigan sweaters. I save money from my disappointing paychecks to purchase CDs. The so-called "Sweater Song" on the *Blue Album*, reminiscent of the college rock I consumed through the 80s, never squared in my head that I liked a band known as Weezer. "Undone", or that so-called "Sweater Song", perfectly captured a mixture of malaise and ennui, its basic chords punctuating my transformation from late youth to working stiff. I hated my job and "Undone" became my commute to work anthem—my messenger bag with brown-bagged lunch inside listening in on the passenger seat.

Only on the rides back home would I sing along to the infectiously poppy "Buddy Holly," an upbeat working girl tribute to Mary Tyler Moore. I could fling my beret—of which I had several—into the skyline and believe for a moment I was *gonna make it after all*. It was a respite from my reality, but I didn't work for Mr. Grant at the local news show in Minneapolis. I lived in Indianapolis and worked for a smug and smarmy boss who posted all important work memos about the urinals in the men's room.

Weezer, as it turns out, became the exact band I needed to help me see that, and even though I had a knack for snappy, sexy ad copy, my current career path would never make me happy. It would take a few more years to get the guts to chuck it and admit to wanting to be a writer—something I'd never utter. Yet in those early years of hand-me-down furniture, milk crates of CDs, Douglas Coupland novels, and Chunky Soup dinners, I dared to dream about an alternate future. The sun would set on

Indy as I scrawled terrible short stories into white composition notebooks at $0.99 a pop.

Say it ain't so but it was.

I stuck with Weezer through better jobs, at least in pay, from the *Blue Album* to the *Green Album*, then *White Album*, and all the ones in between. But enter fourteen-year-old Mary's Twitter feed and her simple mention of a song and band that should have faded with the 1980s.

~

Returning from an academic conference with my friend and program chair Evan, we eat at a diner in BWI airport with surprisingly good food even during an excruciatingly long layover. I am wearing a cardigan sweater, which I button against the artificial chill of HVAC. He's munching on fish-n-chips while I do my best to slaughter a bowl of fried chicken mac-n-cheese. We're headlong into a perpetual conversation about music when Evan articulates a truth about 1980s tunes that cuts me like a dull knife.

"In the 1980s," Evan says, "I was such a snob about music. I like so many more songs from the 80s now than when they came out." This is how nostalgia works, and I can only agree with Evan because it's true of me too. I thought I had moved beyond my snobbishness though.

Except fourteen-year-old Mary uses Twitter to implore Weezer to cover "Africa" by Toto, the sort of soft rock, pop group that defies my overblown nostalgia. Weezer could have saved the song from its faux, contemplative lyrics and problematic geographic references, its "blessing of rains" and Velveeta cheesiness with an edge, through an ironic, pop-punk rendition—sped up and stripped down like a one-night stand.

But, no.

Weezer covers "Africa" with note-for-note fidelity, sincere right down to the 80s synth that might have otherwise gone the way of parachute pants and Hypercolor t-shirts. I felt baffled and betrayed, but worst of all I *keep listening* to it, in thrall of the clear beauty in Rivers Cuomo's vocals. It's as if, in some alternate, bizarro universe, Weezer might make me like "Africa", accepting it as some kind of sonic wonder. *Say it ain't so*, until of course, I accept *the world has turned left me here.*

What drives us to nostalgia? I feel the grip of the past loosen as memories fade like jeans washed too many times—pictures fuzzy at the edges, blurred. Some scar faded from living through it. *The drums echo in the night—* Toto via Weezer, 25 via 45, the long stretch of I-70 east until the cut south into West Virginia. It rains here all the time, and God knows we could use a blessing, rain or otherwise. But I love no other rains, no other place like this one. *Gonna take some time*, I contemplate, *to do the things I never have.* Not such a bad hook. Weezer plays from the patio, as I spend a summer-like day at my house, in this place I've chosen to live. And it's been here in West Virginia longer than any other. Here's your life, girl. The place you have imagined.

You still have all the music and cardigan sweaters.

JAMES KING
TO THE WASP NEST ON THE ELECTRICAL BOX

in what way did a seashell
belong on the kitchen counter
couldn't
              tell you then I left
went out in the world appreciating
the rarity of a good sweat
in October and
when I saw you I laughed
at the unusualness of you
clung
              to a telephone pole
like a little ball of cement
call me morbid call me
sadistic but I couldn't
help but imagine your little guys
inside chewing
on a spark and becoming
impromptu fireflies at
nighttime letting the whole street
see
       your light

MICHAEL CHANG
HIGH DRAMA PANDA FURY

For Blake

A fougère is a scent designed to mimic how a fern smells
Easy, obvious, straightforward enough, except ferns don't really have smells
So a fougère is someone's IDEA of what a fern OUGHT to smell like
. . . nobody dies in this poem b/c dying is not cute
Not all boys are worth chasing
I want to be ambitious yet cowardly
Yes it is better to lie in wait
You are cordially invited to cuddle with me
I want to have nice legs
I want to be tired after practice
I want to have muscles shapely & intimidating
I want to arouse envy
I want to taste artificially flavored blueberry
I want to have never seen Jurassic Park
I want to be unburdened by the knowledge of Jeff Goldblum as sex symbol
I want to be relieved that Chris Pratt is str8
I want to be from Long Island
I want to brunch with Her Majesty's Most Loyal Opposition
I want to catfish the Lieutenant Governor of California
I want to discuss the lady ghostbusters with my lady lawyer
I want to write a poem abt a horse
I want to know where to hide a body
I want to be lost at sea
I want to be one with the otters
I want to speak one language
I want to be Alan Cumming's bathrobe
I want to catch the burglar in the act
I want to kiss him mid-tantrum
I want to call in a favor with the moon
I wonder why ppl don't ask for help
I mean look at you
You clearly need a lot of it

lying in bed at night the pitch of a poem passed through
me
likely not suddenly even though it sure felt like it at the
time
like a prayer in its desire to reach someone

waiting for when the able body & mind had a moment
like this of surrender to stare into the void of all internal
chatter
like an animal not human not hoping of gaining nor
wanting

and here just after midnight in rural Idaho I heard
the words and lines to that good poem
even worthwhile enough to get out of bed right then and
there

LEEOR MARGALIT
ASHES

I wish I were the cigarette
performing the balancing act
so delicately between your lips.
Oh, to live in that house
made of cupped hands
to protect me from the wind
so that the fire catches.
On one end teeth,
on the other, flame
and I, somewhere in the middle—
slowly reduced to ash
with my tangible lifespan.
I linger on you,
a ghost of smoke
on your clothes
in your hair
under your skin.

Last night I prepared for my first real date with a woman as a man. It didn't really start out that differently from the dates I had before I transitioned. I still wonder what I ought to wear, just figuring out how to wear it well in this new-everyday body. I didn't get to the place we were meeting twenty minutes early like I used to, less because my anxiety has decreased and more because I've better learned how to tamper it. I haven't figured out how to stop seeing most things through a gendered lens. If I want a martini or a strawberry margarita, I don't hesitate to order it, but I do poke fun at "the man with the girl drink", even though I don't think my order says anything about my gender; that doesn't stop me from wanting to protect myself from the people that do.

My favorite part was when we talked about music. I fall into a familiar comfort, leaning back against the brick wall of the building and ask her if the Ani Defranco show was full of 40-something women with tribal band tattoos in a sea of bra-less freedom. She laughs and I know that because she knows that community was… is…. Was my community, the playful jest is on the surface of a deep gratitude for the rockin' mommas that showed us the way.

I don't have to wonder at the things she likes and I don't have to wonder at the things I do either. She already knows I was born in the lesbian community, even if many now regard me as their bastard son. She doesn't seem to care about that part, but she doesn't ask questions about it either. For a moment on this date with a stranger, I can wax poetic about Tegan & Sara and stroke my beard at the same time, and I feel incredibly seen. Like the masks we all place on ourselves and one-another are tossed aside for a conversation of just being, and the subsequent sense of belonging it provides me in a moment outside presumed gender.

On the walk home I reflected on how calm I felt. I mozied my way from the subway, glancing up at the lamplight cascading down the tree branches like champagne. I was so drunk on my comfort it took me a minute to notice a woman that I'd been walking behind.

She occasionally looked over her shoulder in my direction as we walked down the dark street—her pace quickening slightly. I knew that behavior. I've felt the tension in my shoulders so many times, and knew well what it was that she was responding to: The moment so many of us raised as women are taught to prepare ourselves for—the moment when our dignity is strapped to our feet, when our intuition of knowing when to run is our only protection.

I moved to the side so I was better in her line of sight and was relieved when I saw the entrance of my building. I planned to make extra noise as I turned up the corridor so that she could know she was safe. Instead she turned into the same walkway of the building and I hesitated to follow, but eventually did. I pulled out my keys hoping the clinking would let her know I was just a tenant, but when she marched to the front door and turned to face me, her eyes wide and staring, hands clutching mace, I knew my plan hadn't worked.

I looked down and to the left and turned my right palm slowly toward her like an offering.

"Woah, hey, I'm sorry. I didn't mean to startle you—I swear I'm not creeping up on you—I just live here."

I pulled up my keys, like *See?*

She apologized profusely, like she was afraid I was going to be angry with her. The fear in her voice overwhelmed me with sadness. I gazed off into the distance and told her it was OK, that it wasn't her fault.

As I walked toward my door she hollered "I'm sorry" at my back again.

"It's O.K.—I get it"

I could hear my voice echoing off the marble halls of the lobby.

"I get it better than you know."

TIMOTHY DODD
CITY LIMITS

The pacifier lies
on downtown asphalt,
melting into the pavement.

Newscasters read
of intersection spinouts,
car crashes, salvaged

androgyny and lost cameras,
then cut to cute commercials
hailing Huggies. Rock doves

have acclimated, but gargoyles
and gods are gone. Mastodons
can't marry Food Lion

and Piggly Wiggly. Hades
heats; my liver riot-rusts,
waiting for beautiful ruins.

LINDSAY MCLEOD
POLES APART

I have stored the magics, tasted the lean hunger in
the air around my wishes. That hint of hope on her

breath when she let me help blow out her candles.
The face on the coin flicked to the all well and good

and how she wagged its tail. The posted prayers I heard
echo all around the sacred chambers of the temple.

The messages skywritten in trails of falling stars, feeling
all those words in Brailleway. The humming of the halo of

her heart and the library of all the words in its murmur.
These glory boxes now full, padded deep to keep me safe

from their kick of reminisce. And yet… I know it's my
own heart that will kill me, again and again and again.

WHAT I SAID HIKING A SLOT CANYON IN BIG BEND RANCH STATE PARK

1. What do you mean there are no bathrooms?

2. I have never pooped in the wilderness, babe, I can hold it.

3. Maybe I can use one of Finn's diapers to catch it?

4. What if I'm mid squat, and a scorpion crawls up my leg and into my vagina. It could happen.

5. Scorpios never liked me.

6. Am I supposed to dig a hole? How do I aim for that? I've never had to aim my bodily excretions before.

7. I know I should not have eaten the burrito, but the cumin tempted me.

8. This is worse than the time I had to sleep in a bathroom with a bullfrog.

9. When I talked about building memorable family experiences, squatting in the only slot canyon in Texas, hoping my bowels don't echo through the top and alert a predator of my vulnerability is not the defining moment of the trip I expected.

10. This place is beautiful.

11. I managed to not poop on my shoe.

12. It's time I become comfortable with life's raw moments.

M. SPENCES-LEE

IMPOSTER

East Toronto is home, Scarborough to be exact. Anyone originally from Toronto hears the word Scarborough and it scares them. Yeah, typically I fit the Scarborough stereotype, as in, if you're a person of colour from Scarborough, you're likely from a low income area, which, in my case, is true but that doesn't define me. In fact, I'm not quite sure what defines me because I've never had the chance to figure it out.

Being from Canada is interesting. Such a young country flooded with immigrants. It's a cultural hub filled with freedoms I would've never been allowed if I was born in my parents' respective countries. Though all 'Canadians' hail from a different place, and I say all because the home we now call Canada was arguably stolen/borrowed/bought, there is still a sense of ethnic hierarchy. If your background is English, Irish, Scottish, Welsh—there is no question of your Canadian roots. This thought is embedded in the culture.

At a young age I was constantly questioned. "Where are you *really* from?" Delving deep into the explanation of how I ended up being born in Canada left me wondering if I even knew the answer to the question. My mother, second generation from a country that she proudly represents, has little connection to it due to genocide. My father, a strong man that carries his West African roots through his flawless night-sky skin, rarely speaks of his patchy heritage due to worldwide enslavement. With such complex backgrounds, my parents were taught upon immigrating to assimilate, but how was/am I expected to identify? Where *am I* really from? What defines me?

I have no idea.

Currently in my thirties, I am still struggling with this question both externally and internally. Our dismissive subtle racism, which is embedded in the way we think, has become known globally, seeping itself overseas. As an avid traveler, I'm constantly interrogated when identifying my birthplace, as if it couldn't be true. I've gone on a personal pilgrimage trying to find any information I can about my lineage. Travelling from country to country in hopes to feel some sort of connection to anywhere else, only to realize my only connection is to Canada.

I was raised in a place where school trips to the ice rink were obligatory—where nature was always accessible. Where any cuisine can be found, where any given day you can hear three languages in one household, where information is attainable—a place where camping is a part of the school curriculum. I grew up alongside families proudly identifying as First Nation, embracing me in all my confused identity despite their own oppression. I grew up liking pineapple on pizza, macaroni and cheese out of a box, and drizzling maple syrup out of a can.

I grew up Canadian.

I grew up questioning my identity due to societal and systematic racism. Now that I'm grown, though still mildly grappling with my identity, I know that where I was nurtured, where I first experienced nature, is where I'm *really* from.

BENJAMIN BARTU
ROAM

from the deli,

boiled spinach stuffed so thick between loaves
the bread disappears in your mouth.

    whatever the sky is searching for, we are already here. i wish
you wouldn't make fun of the couples renting boats

in twenty minute slots to circumnavigate

        the goose-infested

waters; don't you know i wish that was us. or how i know
i am silly for wishes. if the universe

we live in were one in which you liked to do that sort of thing,

pull or be pulled by oar through water, flecks of starch and green
on the surface of the pond, in the gaps between our teeth,

    well. it wouldn't have been you. but a close approximation,

closer to me and farther from you, which, anyway, seems to me
what i had been unfair about for all those years.

never mind that now we can't be close. don't leave me

when you leave me, asking the horse-skins
            where you went in the museum.

Maybe I'm another dead girl,
an electronic billboard flashing
my face between ads for Kroger
and Rent-A-Center. Maybe I'm
the voice in your dreams, the one
that says, Do you ever think of me?
And maybe I'm the wrong turn,
the road you didn't take. Don't worry.
It still had plenty of traffic. And maybe
you're dead, and I am a negative
that nobody bothered to develop.

DR. ALEX VAN HUYNH
PERENNIAL ANNA

All reckonable dyads
In their drywall spaces
Weeping and shuddering by single shared
Lamplight, accusing themselves, self-harming,
And lovemaking when she comes like a child
With quivering lip—this is our living.
On man's only authority,
Leaving her finished and sleeping,
Meteoric streets extend in stillness—
Lifeless midnight, bare illuminations
To walk with that perennial Anna,
Talking of what's done as if it isn't,
And two'd been together
Living forever abroad.

Stopping with her slight anklet of silver
And shells on the sea-smoothed stone,
Pallid legs posing the length of the world,
She begins to give off dreams.

The moon steps down lower
To tide, raising a cold hillside—
Its pale light becoming putrid,
And my mirror-image man
And I slowly touch our lilies,
Unbelieving, yet eyes open
Wilder looks between us—

In his aborted viewing I could see
No authority reflecting upon
The darker and apertural waters,
But her chrysanthemum
Like a great glass skull unwhorling—
Whose shape-shifting child would it be?

In the photograph I appear tall and leggy standing arm in arm with two uniformed gendarmes, one at either side. We're all smiling at the camera, surrounded by palm trees. It's 1975 and I'm wearing a burgundy-colored, hip-length leather jacket tied at the waist, fashionably wide-legged jeans and high-heeled boots. My hair is very long, very straight, and very blonde; in those days I wanted to look like Joni Mitchell. My boyfriend, Michael, whom I met in Paris and would eventually become my first husband, took that picture. I'm around 19 and it's my first trip overseas, studying abroad on a scholarship from a good private college I'd worked hard to get into and even harder to pay for. I think the outfit and the pose make me look older. Or maybe, at that age at that time, we *were* older. Viet Nam. Riots. American cities ablaze. Assassinations. There was Kent State. There were terrors we didn't yet realize. Agent Orange. My cousin Ronnie would one day, many years later, visit the VA hospital trying to get help with that. A farm kid who'd hunted his whole life. They trained him as a sniper.

~

Exposure is determined based on symptoms of the appearance of an official disease. It turns out that, to receive benefits, there needs to be a diagnosed illness specifically identified by the government as associated with Agent Orange.

~

I was eight years old. We were playing King of the Mountain in the hayloft of my aunt and uncle's barn. I usually shied away from games. I didn't know the rules for this one and I was too embarrassed to ask. I was skinny, and bookish, and uncomfortable in my own body. Made King by my cousins, I was immediately pushed off the mountain of hay. I fell through the haymow trapdoor to the concrete floor two stories below. I didn't cry. My cousin Ronnie, then sixteen, picked  me up and carried me into the house. My arm was broken—in three places, though we wouldn't know that for another week. My cousin told the grown-ups that we were all just playing, and I fell. I was an accident. It wasn't anyone's fault.

~

Recently Ronnie sold off most of his cattle. He's spending more time with his wife Cindy who's a cancer survivor. She lived the better part of two years at the University hospital in the Cities where my mother and my older sister would sometimes visit her. The way I hear it she was so ill that no one except Ronnie really believed she could recover. That was some years back and until recently she was working—cooking and baking—for the café inside the Tri-State Auction Barn in Motley, Minnesota, not far from where they both grew up. It burned to the ground a couple of years ago from an electrical fire originating from the kitchen. Fortunately, the building caught fire at night and there were no animals or people inside. It wasn't salvageable, so they've since built a new Sales Barn, though Cindy's not working for them anymore.

~

Ronnie looks in on his Dad pretty regularly, and when the need arises, he also looks after his youngest grandson. He likes taking him ice fishing. Teaching him how to open up the hole and fish with a spear or a line. Showing him how to feed the remaining livestock. Or demonstrating loading up the wood boiler that heats his house.

~

From: *Compensation, Agent Orange Settlement Fund*, U.S. Department of Veterans Affairs: *During the past decade, the Department of Veterans Affairs has received many inquiries regarding the Agent Orange Settlement Fund. That Fund, created as a result of a private class action lawsuit settlement, involved neither VA nor any other executive branch agency of the Federal government. The Settlement Fund closed in 1997. Below is a brief history:*

The Agent Orange Settlement Fund was created by the resolution of the Agent Orange Product Liability Litigation—a class action lawsuit brought by Vietnam Veterans and their families regarding injuries allegedly incurred as a result of the exposure of Vietnam Veterans to chemical herbicides used during the Vietnam war. The suit was brought against the major manufacturers of these herbicides. The class action case was settled out-of-court in 1984 for $180 million dollars, reportedly the largest settlement of its kind at the time.

Applications for the Payment Program had to be submitted prior to December 31, 1994. To be eligible for compensation under the Payment Program, Vietnam Veterans or their survivors had to establish the following:

- that the Veteran served in Vietnam as a member of the Armed Forces between 1962 and 1972 (the period during which Agent Orange was used in Vietnam);

- that the applicant was either a totally-disabled Vietnam Veteran or the survivor of a deceased Vietnam Veteran;

- that based upon the circumstances of the Veteran's service (including location of service and particular experiences during service), the Veteran met a test of probable exposure to herbicides;

- that death or disability was not caused by a traumatic or accidental occurrence; and

- that death or disability occurred before December 31, 1994.

~

He sent the photograph I'd asked him for. They arrived wrapped inside a folded, hand-written letter—plainly penned in ballpoint on faintly blue-line stationary—tucked in a small envelope with a cancelled Purple Heart

postage stamp in the corner. Thepictures in faded Kodacolor show my cousin sometimes alone, sometimes with other young men—posing in the middle of war materiel: guns and sandbags and helicopters and machinery. He writes, *I found some pictures of my service days but none in my uniform when I was young. I guess I never took any thinking I was done with it all. The gun is a 102 Howitzer—the helicopter is a CH 47. That is how we moved. Below the gun is a A-22 bag that held our belongings. We also hauled ammo this way as well as water in a tank on a trailer. The red clay in Viet –Nam turned everything red or deep orange. I hope I have explained things so you understand how it was. My time in Viet –Nam was January '70 to March of '71.*

~

From a towering stainless-steel pole in his front yard, Ronnie flies the POW/MIA banner hung beneath an enormous American flag. In recent year, he's heard there's almost no chances at all there are still POWs in country. Or that there are any unknown MIAs, though the government admits that the bodies of 1200 men killed in action are still uncovered. Ronnie's active in the local VFW Post, but his dad—my uncle Herb—who volunteered for service in WWII, has never chosen to be involved. Herbie was a farmer all his life. They wanted him to continue to farm for the war effort, but, he said, everyone else was going. He was just 18 and he wanted to go too. He joined the Navy. Said he thought the food would be better and he'd have his own bed to sleep in. He served three years on an ammunition ship—the Rainier—in the South Pacific. When I lived in D.C., I would often walk down to the Mall. Shortly after its construction was completed, I strolled around the new WWII memorial with its bronze laurel wreaths mounted on fifty-six granite pillars—one for every state and protectorate—its illuminated rainbow pool and waterworks, and the imposing pavilions, paired at either end of the plaza to commemorate the two theatres of the war: the Atlantic and the Pacific. Later I asked my uncle if he would ever want to come out East and see it He'd been in it, he said, no need to visit a monument to it.

~

My cousin's never been out of the country since he came home. Arriving back in the States, in uniform, he was jeered and cursed at. He says he can certainly see now why people were upset. But he didn't understand why at the

time. He'd been away two tours and they didn't hear much about home over there, except what was going on right there. Ronnie's 72 now and recently asked my husband for help with the Purple Heart. There was the jungle and a firefight and a guy he didn't know cradling his severed leg in his arms, as the wounded were medivacked out by helicopter. Later, Ronnie woke up in an unmarked tent surrounded by Vietnamese. He didn't know if he was a prisoner or a patient or both. He needed surgery but he was afraid of anesthesia. Afraid he'd be injected by the enemy. Afraid he'd never wake up. In the middle of the procedure, looking around, he though he recognized some other American soldiers and he figured he was safe.

~

Turns out there needs to be an officer's statement, a doctor's report logged on-site describing the wound and how it was sustained, and a certified record of subsequent treatment—a raft of official documentation on file alongside supporting paperwork that needs to be submitted and investigated. At the time, he didn't want to make a big deal out of it. He didn't feel right about it. It wasn't that bad for him. And he knew he'd be OK.

JESSICA T. BROWN
READY

I've come to wonder
If all of life's plunders
Are products of patriarchy
And white supremacy

Why else would I
Doubt my skin
Pick and prick
At my beauty within

Why else would I
Allow others to say
How I should
Be shaped and swayed

No longer am I
Bound by realities
Built by racists
Meant to trap me

ESTHER HSU
PEACE/LESS/LILIES

When I was small, I took classes about plants.
I lost everything save for the 3 necessities—
carbon dioxide, water, and photosynthesis.

Carbon dioxide
is your life;
monoxide, your poison,
a slow, lonely prison.

But it is my life
line the inside of my throat,
searing the remains of your
breath asphyxiating mine and
beautifully breaking dicarbon union.

You are no longer the
water necessary for my photosynethe
cis-gender white girl (over)shadows light,
burns a picture perfect polaroid photo
synthesis of savior complex and ignorance and bigotry,
big white tree snuffs out sun with supremacy.

I offer you
white peace
lilies aka spath;
little do you know of
your senseless path
your beloved white (oxalade) skin,
spathiphyllus stem
are
Note:
            toxic,
            causes skin irritation and
            burning sensation in mouth.

Causes carbon dioxide deficiency,
causes the light you never had
to perish.

When we broke up,
I regained everything—
monoxide, blood, and   peace /lilies/.

This is it. There's no turning back. Do you think my Uber driver knows what's about to happen?... How long does it take to get around this city anyway? Am I doing the right thing? No. Am I doing the wrong thing?...

Wait.
Better to back up.
Back to the first text.
Rewind.

Dec. 1, 2017
Him. 11:52 p.m.: Everything ok with Molly?

He texted me. I didn't think he was going to text me. I mean, he took a selfie of us and Riley on his phone, and I (devilishly) told him to send it to me. "I don't have your number," he said, and I gave it to him. But to use it again? This soon, minutes after Riley's party? Is this normal? What do I say?

Me. 11:53 p.m.: As far as I know yeah, Sean has it handled and her boyfriend is heading to her place
I still have her purse lol, which smells of vomit
You get home ok?

Molly is going to love this. She championed this hook-up. She was there every time he put his hand on my back and shoulder, every time we poured more and more red wine into his cup. She was there for me then and is there for me now, even though the wine got the best of her—and her purse.

Him. 11:54 p.m.: Oh my. Yes just got back

I thought Molly's vomit ended the night. Is this just the beginning?

Me. 11:54 p.m.: Ya quite eventful
Ah ok good!

Him. 11:57 p.m.: You?

"You". He cares. One word, but there's so much packed in it. You is me and you is you, and you and me is us.

Me. 11:58 p.m.: Almost, in an Uber. She's playing 2010s pop, we understand each other

Do <u>we</u> understand each other?

Him. 11:59 p.m.: Oh wow good for you

Good for you. Good for me.

Dec. 2, 2017
Him. 12:01 a.m.: Heading home

Is that a question? I think it's a question.

Me. 12:04 a.m.: Haha yeah lucked out. Ok now officially home. Any plans or you done for the night

Him. 12:05 a.m.: Partyin with wine solo for the moment

For the moment. Is that an invitation? Maybe I should wait longer between texts. Molly would tell me to wait longer between texts.

Me. 12:11 a.m.: Heh cute

Fuck. No response.

Me. 12:13 a.m.: What are you drinking

Him. 12:14 a.m.: Finishing a merlot
You?

Whew. Let's get to it. Is this happening? Am I going to make this happen? Is tonight the night?

Me. 12:15 a.m.: Haven't found anything to satisfy me yet.

Boom.

Him. 12:16 a.m.: Oh

That's right.

Me. 12:19 a.m.: But the night isn't necessarily over

Him. 12:19 a.m.: Whys that

Quick on the text trigger now, aren't you?

Me. 12:21 a.m.: I could stay awake a little longer if I had someone to hang out with

Him. 12:23 a.m.: Ha you sound tired

He's correct. This is way past my bedtime. But goddamnit, if I'm going to lose my virginity tonight, I will not let this thwart my plans. Does he know? Is he teasing me? Is this a game? What do I—

Me. 12:25 a.m.: ¯_(ツ)_/¯ eh, a second wind is inevitably coming

Him. 12:25 a.m.: Nice!
My prob is I changed out of pants

Me. 12:27 a.m.: Same, but that's not really a problem

Boom.

Him. 12:27 a.m.: haha good attitude

What are you, my camp counselor? You're old enough to have been, I guess.

Me. 12:28 a.m.: I like to think so. Any other fun plans this weekend?

Him. 12:29 a.m.: Supposed to hang with a buddy tomorrow and then drinks Sunday
But we'll see
You?

Aha, so he's malleable.

Me. 12:30 a.m.: Working on a freelance piece tomorrow and Sunday, and the Salvation Army is coming by at some point to pick up our old futon. Otherwise pretty open

Open.

Him. 12:30 a.m.: Busy

Me. 12:30 a.m.: Busy-ish, depends how fruitful my reporting goes. But nights are free

Take the hint, my dude.

Him. 12:31 a.m.: Cool. Didn't realize how early it was tonight

Me. 12:31 a.m.: This still early for you?

Fuck. Now he knows.

Him. 12:31 a.m.: Ha yeah
I'm a night owl
Not you?

Not you. Not me. Not you and not me. Not us.

Me. 12:32 a.m.: I'm typically more of an early bird but can be persuaded otherwise

Him. 12:32 a.m.: Look at you

Look at me.

Me. 12:33 a.m.: Heh I'm more than what people bargain for

Him. 12:33 a.m.: Aren't we all

We. Us.

Me. 12:34 a.m.: We're all just pantsless drinking wine by ourselves
    12:35 a.m.: Metaphorically and literally

Him. 12:35 a.m.: Haha Pantless is good

Me. 12:35 a.m.: I prefer it

Him.: ~likes~ "I prefer it"

Me. 12:39 a.m.: I'm now drinking water because I don't want tomorrow to be hellish

Him. 12:39 a.m.: Professional

Me. 12:39 a.m.: Too responsible for my own good

Him. 12:39 a.m.: Im the opposite

Dare I make the pun. I'll do it. I have nothing to lose. Rather, everything.

Me. 12:41 a.m.: Heh opposites attract
      12:42 a.m.: Damn I'm sorry That was a terrible line

Him. 12:42a.m.: You're fine
I'm just hangin

Same. Let's do it together?

Me. 12:42 a.m.: I will take that for all its meanings
      12:43 a.m.: Lol

Him. 12:43 a.m.: Oh

What? What does "oh" mean?

Me. 12:43 a.m.: Unless I shouldn't

Him. 12:43 a.m.: ?

I have no idea what is happening now.

Me. 12:44 a.m.: Nvm

Him. 12:45 a.m.: Oh

…I'm calling this one. DOA.

Me. 12:48 a.m.: I'm probably gonna fall asleep soon. But
talk to you later

12:49 a.m.: Pantsless or not

Him. 12:49 a.m.: Tonight?

…or maybe not.

Me. 12:49 a.m.: Haha are you staying up all night?

Him. 12:50 a.m.: Maybe lol
1936 11th St

!!! There's that invitation.

Me. 12:49 a.m.: See you soon

Him. ~emphasizes~ "See you soon"

You. Me. My Uber driver. This is it. There's no turning back. Do you think my Uber driver knows what's about to happen? That 25+ years of anticipation are about to boil over in some dude's apartment? How long does it take to get around this city anyway? Am I doing the right thing? No. Am I doing the wrong thing? No. I'm not in love. I thought I was going to be in love, thought I was supposed to be in love. I'm in lust and that is OK. I want him and he wants me and I love that. I love me.

Him. 1:08 a.m.: Oh

Oh not now, I'm having a damn moment.

Me. 1:08 a.m.: Lol
Momentarily

Him. 1:09 a.m.: Jk jk

Here we go.

Me. 1:10 a.m.: Here

…help.

Him. 1:13 a.m.: ?

Dude. I'm not going to wait forever and make awkward eye contact with this receptionist who definitely thinks I'm doing the wrong thing.

Me. 1:15 a.m.: *Eyeroll emoji*

Him. 1:15a.m.: Huh

1:17 a.m.: 617

Up I go.

THALIA GEIGER
JUDGEMENT DAY

I wonder about you if another lump grew back and about
the word remission the transience that's part of it and you finally

text me back say no you're just busy so I say oh. and okay.
but with the orange skies and the way the world's been I have a right

to worry don't I? wasn't Jesus supposed to be here by now?
I look for the bearded fellow we all once believed in but outside

across the street from my house I just see a white gleam flash
by with the chime of a Mr. Softee truck. soon the children

will be here and I'll want to go. if you had asked me how
I've been I would've said I just stick on lots of fake tattoos because

I don't have anyone to touch me. now I have two tattoos so
I feel like I'm always being touched and though I don't work I

work hard to cleanse everything so I can be pure and at ease.
I throw your sweater in the trash can so I don't get gasoline all over

my back patio. a little witchcraft and I have our eight years of friendship
inside a tiny bottle with that perfume we both liked, salt, nails,

lemon juice, the works. when I shake it vigorously I wonder if you're
alerted to the white noise buzzing in your ear. I wonder if you think it's
Him.

Roger was fading.

Six people were in Gloria's communication node and she didn't care a fig for five of them.

But she cared for Roger.

It wasn't a crush—she was far too reasonable for that. It would be ridiculous to fall for a randomly assigned correspondent that you knew nothing about. Where he lived, what he did, if somebody else lived in that apartment, of which she never saw more than a sofa, an armchair, a window in the back that might, or might not, have a view of the sea. It was the window that caught her interest—well before she noticed that Roger had a slightly lopsided smile, an unruly mop of hair, and very clear blue eyes. He moved slowly, as if distracted by things on his mind that he was trying to sort out. He was never in a hurry to get out of the spying eye of the home capture camera. The other members of the node were constantly flitting in and out of the frame, impatient and purposeful. Gloria knew their names but they were never on screen long enough for her to get a good look at them. She doubted she could pick them out of a line-up. Not that she would ever be asked. What could she tell about these people? They were strangers when she moved into the apartment and six months later they still were.

Gloria couldn't remember a time when there were no node companions. The artificial and shallow comradeship was a given, it came with the rental agreement or the mortgage. You neither had a choice of who to include in your assigned node, nor the ability to remove or tune out any of them. In theory, you could add friends and family if you were willing to pay for the extra connections.

Short of sticking a piece of cardboard over the screens, the images were always present. A small label affixed to the wall informed the occupant of the house or flat that tampering with the node was a misdemeanor, which would be subject of prosecution. The penalty—a fine, jail time—was not specified. Fighting the screens was pointless anyway. Just leave the room or, simply, close your eyes.

Node participants could interact with each other—it was highly recommended—but nobody ever did. Perhaps people used to have conversations when the screens were first installed but the need wore away with time.

"Refresh," Gloria said.

The images folded up and for a couple of seconds the wall screen was a restful, uniform gray, until the pictures scrolled up again. Coralee was first to appear in the bottom right corner, then Lewis bottom left, and all the way up to Roger, top left. He was still blurry—more so than before. Gloria was aware of the irony. For six months she had stared at the image of this man, contemplated contacting him, but did not. And now that he might disappear, she was all aflutter.

Gloria pushed the transmitter output button for number six. Her finger trembled. She had never initiated a conversation. She took a deep breath and rushed through the words. "Coralee? I'm having trouble with Roger's transmission. He's in slot number one for me; he's all fuzzy. Do you have the same problem?"

A long, long silence. Was Coralee shocked out of her wits to hear sound coming from the video wall? "Uh, yes." The voice was tinny, traveling all the way from the end of a long tunnel.

"Okay, thanks. Sorry I disturbed you." Click. She would have to bite the bullet and call Roger. Something must be wrong with the video feed on his end. Her hand hovered over the transmitter.

"Roger? It's Gloria." She took a raspy breath. She was seeing bright dots and feared she might faint, like a hoop-skirted heroine in a Romantic novel. She pulled herself together. "Your transmission is fading. You should call tech support."

There was no response. Maybe the vaunted node technology was just a clunky patched-together low-speed network. It looked advanced but rusty cogs clanked in the background. "Sorry," Roger said. "I'm on it." Another lengthy pause. "Thanks."

He had a pleasantly deep voice, warm, not at all like Coralee's. Gloria wanted to continue the conversation, but he slipped out of the screen. Then, just like that, the image disintegrated in a shower of glittering pixels. Gone. She sat on the sofa, feeling exhausted. He said he was on it and sounded competent. He would be back, she was certain of it. Gloria tore herself away from the screens. It was late.

~

"She's in distress. We're losing her."

"For chrissake, Tilly, it's just a string of code!"

"Right. Sure." Tilly had been tinkering with the software for twenty straight hours and the strain was showing. She was irritated with everything and barked at everyone. "I don't know what to do. I tried every procedure at least twice. She's not responding."

Five years on the project, with setbacks and small victories, and then the breakthrough with Gloria. Everybody believed it would be smooth sailing from that point on. No more dogged groundwork, no more heavy coding. The basics were sound. They were in the fine-tuning phase now, making small changes to the algorithms to test the program's flexibility. Gloria always adjusted nicely to the minute modifications and her learning loop worked even better and faster than expected. The project was a definite success—until last night, when Gloria went dark.

"Have you walked back the most recent changes?" Roger said.

"What do you think I've been doing?" Tilly grabbed a pack of cigarettes sticking out from the pocket of his lab coat. *The hell with the rules.* Let the sprinklers douse her. The way management scrounged at every corner, she doubted the damn things were even connected to the water line. She held a hand out for a lighter, and pushed a worksheet toward Roger. "Here they are. Every single little tweak we made to her core over the past week. I backtracked every line of code. No dice. Gloria's gone off to a place I can't reach and I don't know what caused it. It's like…a psychotic break or something."

"I wish you didn't make it so personal. You're freaking me out. Psychotic, Jesus, Tilly! We wrote code, we didn't give birth to a child! You remember how Marshall looked at you when you slipped and called it Gloria in the oral review? The sponsors were squirming in their seats. I thought they would bolt out of the door and holler for the medics to come in with the straitjackets."

Tilly tilted her chair until it hit the back wall. She was furious, mostly because Roger was right. She made it too personal. She lived inside that computer with Gloria. And she didn't know how to do her job any other way. "All right. *Gamma Latent Operating Response Artificial Intelligence,* G.L.O.R.A.I. went for a hike and wandered off the trail. Suggestions? Should we send a search party?"

Roger plucked the cigarette from her fingers and crushed it in her empty in-tray. It made a melted dent in the cheap plastic. "You're too tired to think straight. It… Gloria …" He shrugged.

"Give me a break. We all use pet names. Brian names his rats and performs funerals when one of them passes."

"Brian is a nutcase. Put your anxieties on hold for a minute and think. Gloria didn't run away from home after a spat with mom. Something interfered with the programming and caused a glitch. We built it, we can fix it. What about sleep mode? We've rebooted before and the sequence always kicked back to initial settings. It's time consuming but we won't lose anything."

Tilly sighed. She handed him the VR helmet and gloves. "See for yourself." She watched him plug in. Roger's blue eyes behind the visor assumed the familiar faraway stare of the roamer. She saw his expression change. Surprise, disbelief, a touch of fear. He took the helmet off. He was a little pale.

"You still think it's just code?" Tilly said. "Something we can erase and no harm done? An entry on a time sheet? All the steps are documented. If we work fast, Marshall won't even notice the delay. Right?" Tilly was vindicated by the look on his face.

He pulled off the gloves, putting them in the helmet and carefully deposited the VR set on the lab bench. "We can't do that. It would be wrong, like…" He got a cigarette from the pack and lit it. "It's a complete mess." He ran his fingers through his floppy hair and coughed. "It's disturbing to see it, uh, her, like that. So utterly miserable. It's so…real." He looked lost. "That visual interface packs a punch."

Tilly felt a surge of affection for him, a tenderhearted mathematician. She took the VR helmet and shook out the gloves. "I'm into this so much, I tend to forget what we're here to do. She's my girl, Rog. I can truly say that I know her inside out. I'll give it another go. Would you mind getting me a coffee?"

When Roger came back, Tilly was scrolling through stacks of code. "Who took out the wall screen?"

"The what?"

"The node. The interaction loop we put in at the very beginning. After we went to that lecture on the socialization of children. How a group setting enhances learning."

"Ah. I took it out. Marshall was looking for ways to trim the budget and simplify the software. The node wasn't used anyway. There was never any contact from … Gloria." Roger sighed. He was still having trouble with the name. "She never called any of the avatars."

"Then what is that?" Tilly pointed at a series of blinking lines on her screen. It was a rhetorical question. They both read the code as easily as plain English. "She responded logically. The wall was a fixture in her environment. When the deletion started, she wanted the images restored."

For years Tilly had nurtured Gloria, from basic stimulus-response mechanisms to increasingly more nuanced reactions in an effort to reproduce emotions that were as close as possible to their human equivalent. Teaching an AI takes time but the process isn't inherently complex. It's a matter of data accumulation and conditional rules. Teaching it to feel, however, is an elusive pursuit. They had been fooled a few times into believing that G.L.O.R.A.I. had made an emotional jump when it had simply applied a particularly convoluted logical sequence. It wasn't empathy, just advanced math. They had even joked that the programming was so intricate that their creation made quite the fine sociopath.

"It could be a case of conflicting instructions," Roger said. "The wall screen should work and it doesn't. She uses the options at her disposal and none of them delivers the expected result. Hence, trouble."

"Mishaps have thrown her into a spin before and her processes froze. She never started *crying*, Rog. I think you broke her heart."

He made a little dismissive gesture. "Let's not be melodramatic. I deleted a few files. I'll plug them back in. Marshall can go look somewhere else for his cost cutting." He took a sip of the coffee Tilly hadn't touched. "What now? Why are you looking at me like that?"

"Your avatar was the first to be deleted. I initiated a specific search on a hunch. I bet she spent more time looking at your feed than all the others combined. The girl has good taste." Tilly smiled. "I programmed her."

"That is so disturbing."

"The power of love," Tilly said. "Gloria is starting her emotional journey on a high note. No wonder she's all discombobulated."

Roger shot her a lopsided smile and finished the coffee. "We thought we were dealing with a baby learning steps and now we have a moody teenager on our hands. Let's hope she grows out of it fast."

"I never really did," Tilly said. "Did you?"

JAMES KING
TRUTH IS, THERE IS ONLY ONE MOON

Like all Earthlings after 1969, I feel
left behind   waiting
on a letter

in the black heights   where you go
not even a crinkle
of paper
can be heard

but hey   even the shiest ghosts   long
to be remembered

me   I sizzled dumplings
shining crescents   slippery pan
ate a quiet meal
for one   wasn't enough

every night   one might think
there was a different moon
each a different set
of permanent footprints

tonight   I go to get the mail
I never find the letter
that I want   no different   then
the blizzard eats my soles

you drifting out there somewhere

I come in to
stacks of scribbles on the coffee table
eager with return postage

I have so many answers waiting

JOHN DORROH
"Bird Flu"

You were always among the birds,
standing like a flamingo, waiting
for another storm to bristle your salmon-
pink feathers. We knew where to find
you, stuck in avian dreams of feathery
things, waiting for the ATM to spit
forth a brilliant stack of green. You
missed school and flight and driving
in torrential rains to useless football
games; to block parties where everyone
asked, and then quit asking, "Where's
your dad?" He's got the bird flu again,
unable to hop out of bed, to breathe
unobstructed breaths like a normal man.
We covered for you, we covered you,
with our own special feathers whose
brisk denial wafted up from the dirty
kitchen floor all the way to the top
of your head.

The last time I saw my father was about twenty-five years ago. His house on 820 Cynthia Avenue was situated on the top of a small urban mountain in the northeast armpit of Los Angeles. I barely knew how to get there and it seemed best to veer left and go up, in second gear, past the taco trucks and loud boombox music from the streets. I parked my Buick past the red Toyota pickup truck he once promised me, now rusting in the field. I thought of what it must be like for him to drive past that truck everyday on the way home from teaching.

I was early and my father was late. I came out of the orchard to meet him with a brown grocery bag of avocados, newly picked. His eyes met mine and I saw his jugular vein bulge and his face redden. "You are stealing my avocados," he said. I felt the sick sinking feeling of my heart unraveling like yarn, down, back to my unhinged childhood of helplessness. *What?* I thought. Then I lied and said, "They were on the ground." He said nothing. I tried to speak but the words came out of my mouth and dropped flat in the dry heat of the oppressive afternoon. I said, "I thought it was okay to take some."

"Why would you think that?" I thought: this is your house, this is your land, your trees, your avocados and because I am your daughter. *But I wasn't, not in that moment, and not for so many years.*

~

My father beat my mother and my brothers. My mother would shriek, plead, and there was The Pause—a deafening silence that would envelop me, and protect me from the Other. I smelled warm sticky blood. I hid in the grim narrow kitchen cabinet. I held the broom, trying not to breathe. Through a crack in the door I saw my mother's hand impaled to the wooden kitchen table with a wooden pencil by my father, broken glass littered everywhere.

My father, Peter Parrish, was an Astrophysics graduate student at University of California at Berkeley and he had a daughter from a previous marriage. He wore Patchouli oil on his leather belt and successfully seduced my already married mother by taking her to house parties with philosophers and mathematicians. He told my mother that her given birth name was not Harriet but Heather. He put flowering plants of purple heather up along the staircase of his collegiate communal house.

My mother finally got what she wanted. A baby girl. The marriage ended before it started. He sold her car, changed her name, erased all traces of her first husband's residue, and then proceeded to go after what meant the most to her—to destroy her other three children, to break her. During the beatings, first one then the other, there were screams and then the screaming finally stopped. I remember my life before the age of five—but it comes forth as slivers of pain bubble up. The hot push of bacteria boluses break free and I feel the void, the empty nauseous space of where pain lived for so many decades. I smell the stubborn residue of regret. Blank numb spaces existing between well-rehearsed statements of timelines that don't make sense and have lost meaning.

I don't remember why I went to see my father. Maybe it was to patch things up in my mid-twenties, when I came back from the ashram in OR and went to LA. It was in my calendar, held together with a blue, broccoli rubber band. He was expecting me. It was before emails were a thing. Maybe he had written one of his long letters in cursive on thin paper, folded into four sections that unfolded like accordion or a spring. The edge of the creases were crisp and were pushed flat with a letter knife.

~

I had seen the trunkful of old Kodachrome photographs during my father's fiftieth birthday party— roughly seventy people milling around with Cajun music projecting out of tiny strategic speakers throughout the property. Since I was not drinking the beer and tequila, nor was I interested in dancing with men twice my age, I ended up in the living room where my father once showed me his trunk of photos. I kept sifting through them, photos of me smiling and laughing. I was puzzled. I kept searching through the images which had faded from the sun.

The music pounded, and women twirled by with colorful skirts and long hair through the open, sliding-glass door that led out to the sunbaked patio. But there was nowhere to escape to but these photos.

I was in every one, with freckles and big perfect teeth. There was not one photo where I was not present. How could that be? There was not one perfect photograph—they were all perfect. My father was the one who took all the photographs of our family. He was the one who was in charge of documenting my childhood.

I was too afraid to take a photo with me. I wanted to keep one, but which one? I couldn't pick one anyhow. I would have to ask permission. What if he said no? I was conscious of how long I was looking at the photos. I closed the lid and walked away. Later I would ask my mother, *was I a happy child?* "Yes," my mother told me. "You were the most beautiful baby. I told them they must have been mistaken. You were too beautiful to be mine."

The trunk sat in the middle of my father's living room, where he put his feet up from the deep couch. I thought of him sitting there, lording over his ability to procreate and have two daughters and three wives—patents in physics, doctorate in astrophysics, and his ripening avocados.

I stopped mailing him photos of his grandson. My son stopped asking about the grandfather he has never met. I kept thinking each year I got my tax refund that I would drive down to LA and surprise him.

I wondered if I had siblings now—my father with his new young wife that was only a few years older than his first daughter.

I wondered if COVID would take him away and I would never see the photos of my childhood again.

CHRISTOPHER FARAGO
I Wait

In a bath
of orange and patchouli
I read Oliver and Plath,
each giving their take
on lilies.

I step out of the tub,
and I wait for the water
to freeze over
so I can skate between them.

My hair dries, grays, turns to ash, disappears.

SHAWN ANTO
BONE-STILL LANDSCAPE

I remember the times   when my cousin Tinto and I   would wake up on summer weekends go to
the rice fields   with our coconut-branch bat and tennis ball   play cricket

He'll always be the little master

I would be The Wall

—

now, nobody plays in the fields
or the streets anymore

we emptied them, the kids have emptied them

nobody bothers when they have the neon god at their fingers

our connections, particles of a past we will never get back
sits on the bone

collects

as each swing whips the bails

dormant, another memory   —

all memory of worth suffers in the bone sharpened up, memories are ready for an executioner at the doorstep, masks on cool, collected approach — I finally feel an end, its grave stillness approaching pendulum inched into bone, I would die toward this delicacy, if my name didn't caress its beginning. rough with spare parts, spare me another delusion – this is why my parents never stayed in one place, their names didn't hold any value there, the wooden-stumps never took hold on the ground, everything seemed to dangle, move, shift, at each swing, like a game we played but were always afraid to, to win was a dream, to lose seemed the best route, stuck in the bone until they could saw it out, watch   bone   fall, right in front of them.

BENJAMIN BARTU
THEREWHILE

matching urns open.

before-ash, we.

tumbled across gorse.

in the great variance.

we go.

in life.

a great hotel.

with really long

tibia shaped hallways

you can lap

with me like water.

if you like.

there'll be laughter.

smattering dark purple.

droplets across cloth.

the children we never.

ever have. Jokes.

here's one joke.

alright. you've heard.

of the thigh gap.

but how about.

the empathy gap?

some people

get it.

sides hurt.

in other cities.

i am a hand.

fallen gingerly

over a candle.

i am lucky.

i place a hand.

on me and flicker.

tomorrow gutters.

it gets hotter.

shall i hold you,

webbed planet?

chorus: someone danced,

[con't]: therefore we danced.

certainly.

a world to save.

world to savor.

i'm almost sure of it

ADDITIONAL INFO

Follow us on social media:

@tildeliteraryjournal

@tildelit

/tildelit

Purchase a previous issue of Tïlde~ at:

thirtywestph.com/shop

For full guidelines, submission info, and our online archive, please visit:

thirtywestph.com/tildelit